Tidy Tim

The 'Get to Know Me' series is aimed at children with additional needs and those who support them in the classroom. Developed by child psychologist Dr Louise Lightfoot and illustrated by Catherine Hicks, the resources in this series include activities specific to anxiety, depression and Obsessive Compulsive Disorder (OCD). This book, *Tidy Tim*, has been designed to support the individual child but also to be used in whole class teaching, to encourage an empathetic and inclusive environment.

In this book, we meet Tidy Tim, an octopus with many arms but not many friends. His swirly whirly feelings make him spend all day cleaning and tidying his house instead of going out and making friends. But one day, Tidy Tim gets himself into a terrible tangle and realises he needs the help of Jenni the Jellyfish, who helps him untangle his arms and his feelings.

This book was written with children with OCD in mind, providing an opportunity to relate to Tim's thoughts, feelings, behaviours and experiences. However, children with a range of needs may benefit from the story. The book is written in a narrative style, so it does not use diagnostic labels and is not intended for this purpose. Instead the focus is on creating a common language which children can understand and use to make sense of how they are feeling.

A practitioner guidebook (ISBN 978-0-8153-4948-8) and draw along version (ISBN 978-0-8153-4951-8) are also available.

Dr Louise Lightfoot is an Educational and Child Psychologist working with children and young people aged 0–25. She holds a BA in Educational Studies, MEd in the Psychology of Education and doctorate in Educational and Child Psychology. Louise has worked in a variety of settings ranging from mainstream schools to secure units and psychiatric facilities, and has a special interest in working to empower at risk or 'hard to reach' groups. As a person who suffers with Ehlers Danlos, stroke and dyslexia, she has a first-hand understanding of the frustrations and difficulties that accompany a specific physical or learning difficulty. Louise currently works as an HCPC registered Independent Psychologist. If you would like to discuss working with her, please contact Louise at: louise.lightfoot@hotmail.co.uk

Catherine Hicks is an East Yorkshire artist, illustrator, wife and mother. She spent 13 years as a Registered Veterinary Nurse before injury and chronic illnesses led to her creative hobby becoming therapy. When Catherine and Louise were introduced, it was obvious they were kindred spirits and from there the Get to Know Me Series was born.

GET TO KNOW ME SERIES

Series author: Dr Louise Lightfoot
Illustrated by: Catherine Hicks

The **'Get to Know Me'** series is a series of resources aimed at children with additional needs and the professionals who support them in the mainstream primary classroom. Each resource concentrates on a different condition and comprises of three titles, available separately.

A **traditional children's picture book** – designed to support the individual child but also to be used in whole class teaching, to encourage an empathetic and inclusive environment.

An **interactive workbook**. This is a workbook version of the story in which individual children are encouraged to interact with the story in a creative way – through writing, drawing, scrap booking, collage, activities etc. (templates and cut outs will be made available online). Children are more likely to understand and process information if they have had to actively engage with it. The workbook will aid long-term recall and increase the level of understanding.

A **practitioner guide** created for key adults (teachers, therapists and parents) by a child psychologist, with activities specific to each condition. These activities will link to the books and offer practical tools and strategies to support the child and those around them in addition to the information specific to the condition to improve understanding of a child's needs to promote empathy and acceptance.

https://www.routledge.com/Get-To-Know-Me/book-series/GKM

Books included in this series:

Set 1 Get to Know Me: Anxiety
Available as a set and individual books

Book 1
Supporting Children with Anxiety to Understand and Celebrate Difference
A Get to Know Me Workbook and Guide for Parents and Practitioners
PB 978-0-8153-4941-9
eBook 978-1-351-16492-4

Book 2
Sammy Sloth
Get to Know Me: Anxiety
PB 978-0-8153-4953-2
eBook 978-1-351-16452-8

Book 3
Draw Along With Sammy Sloth
Get to Know Me: Anxiety
PB 978-0-8153-4942-6
eBook 978-1-351-16484-9

Set 2 Get to Know Me: Depression
Available as a set and individual books

Book 1
Supporting Children with Depression to Understand and Celebrate Difference
A Get to Know Me Workbook and Guide for Parents and Practitioners
PB 978-0-8153-4943-3
eBook 978-1-351-16480-1

Book 2
Silver Matilda
Get to Know Me: Depression
PB 978-0-8153-4945-7
eBook 978-1-351-16476-4

Book 3
Draw Along With Silver Matilda
Get to Know Me: Depression
PB 978-0-8153-4946-4
eBook 978-1-351-16472-6

Set 3 Get to Know Me: OCD
Available as a set and individual books

Book 1
Supporting Children with OCD to Understand and Celebrate Difference
A Get to Know Me Workbook and Guide for Parents and Practitioners
PB 978-0-8153-4948-8
eBook 978-1-351-16468-9

Book 2
Tidy Tim
Get to Know Me: OCD
PB 978-0-8153-4950-1
eBook 978-1-351-16460-3

Book 3
Draw Along With Tidy Tim
Get to Know Me: OCD
PB 978-0-8153-4951-8
eBook 978-1-351-16456-6

Tidy Tim

Get to Know Me: OCD

Dr Louise Lightfoot

Illustrated by Catherine Hicks

Routledge
Taylor & Francis Group
LONDON AND NEW YORK

First published 2020
by Routledge
2 Park Square, Milton Park, Abingdon, Oxon OX14 4RN

and by Routledge
52 Vanderbilt Avenue, New York, NY 10017

Routledge is an imprint of the Taylor & Francis Group, an informa business

British Library Cataloguing-in-Publication Data
A catalogue record for this book is available from the British Library

Library of Congress Cataloging-in-Publication Data
A catalog record for this book has been requested

ISBN: 978-0-8153-4950-1 (pbk)
ISBN: 978-1-351-16460-3 (ebk)

Typeset in Stone Informal
by Apex CoVantage, LLC

Dedications

From Louise:

Dedicated to Tim, my true love, who told me when I got sick that if I was to remain bed-bound, he would never leave me. Ah, that's for better for worse I thought, how lucky I am to be loved so unconditionally. Tim then went on to explain he wouldn't mind me being bed-bound because I would make less mess. Thank you for taking care of and believing in me. Who doesn't enjoy being served breakfast in bed whilst simultaneously being hoovered by a handheld Dyson? No crumbies in here thank you very much!

And to Jenni, my first love, a love so pure its essence can only be captured by 90s R&B

Girl you are close to me you're like my mother, Close to me you're like my father, Close to me you're like my sister, Close to me you're like my brother. (We did classics so at this point it was getting a bit Oedipal . . . but it was ok because as it turned out . . .) You are the only one you are my everything and for you this song I sing!

You were back then and remain always willing to help me (thanks for the proof reading!) and I'm so lucky to have the rights to the original Jenni the Jellyfish.

From Catherine:

To Erin and Drew, my amazing children, who have inspired me throughout creating Tidy Tim and been there to give their honest opinion at every stage.

And to my Loving Husband and soulmate for all that he does so that I can do what I do. "He's my lobster".

Contents

Acknowledgements

To Katrina my editor, thank you for taking a chance and sticking with us, especially during our particularly 'imperfectly flawed' moments! You have been a wonderful source of personal support and a professional wisdom.

Professor Kevin Woods for your (I often wondered if misguided) belief in me and continued support. Here's to being a square peg in a round hole.

The University of Manchester and the students of the Doctorate of Educational Psychology Course, in particular Jill and Ben Simpson, for their collaboration, perspective and belief.

Huge thank you for the contributions to: Dr Lindsay 'grammar' Kay, Dr Katie Pierce, Dr Richard Skelton, Dr Rachael Hornsby, Dr Rachel Lyons and Jade Charelson for their professional insight, unwavering friendship, invaluable contribution and time. You really are the Waitrose of Psychologists (quality wise, not overpriced!).

Thank you to all my family and friends who have endured numerous versions of these books and for their support during the periods in which I was very ill and gained tenacity from believing I could make something good come out of it all.

To Erin and Drew for being excellent guinea pigs and the source of great inspiration. To Owen for being a friend to me at 13 and 35 with admittedly slightly improved cooking skills. To Dianne Davies for her experience, support and knowledge of the area which helped more than you could know.

A huge thank you to Tim Watson for your supervision, guidance and support. You have helped me realise my potential when I couldn't see it in myself. You are an excellent critical friend, fountain of knowledge and all round lovely person!

Thanks to Catherine Hicks, my illustrator, the gin to my tonic! Perhaps in finding each other we made two slightly broken people whole.

Thanks for my Dad for always believing in me and constantly filling my freezer and thanks to my big brother John, who annoyed me as a child and who has always been there for me as an adult.

To the Hickling family, I couldn't have wished to marry into a better family, your support love and acceptance of me as a Scouser is forever appreciated.

Thanks to Jonathan Merrett, the copy editor, for his patience and flexibility and to Leah Burton, my Editorial Assistant, for her help along the way.

Finally, a huge thank you to Gillian Steadman, my Senior Production Editor, who is the yin to my yang. Couldn't have done this without you!

Tidy Tim – A picture book story

Deep, deep down in the ocean
Where squishy fishes swim,
Lived many different creatures
And an octopus called Tim.

Tim wasn't very friendly
Or blessed with many charms,
But Tim had lots of other skills
As well as lots of arms.

Tim was super organised
And always had a plan;
His house was very ordered
And always spick and span.

One day a knock came to his door,
He heard a small voice say,
"Hello, Tim – are you in there?
Oh, won't you come and play?"

He looked out of his window
"It's me," a voice declared.
"It's Jenni the jelly fish! Please come play!"
But Tim just stood and stared.

"I'm busy," Tim replied at once
"I've lots of things to do
The house is very messy
I have no time for you"

Jenni asked Tim every day,
Though he never once came out
She'd ask him still, just in case,
And so he wouldn't feel left out.

Jenni turned and swam away
And Tim felt sad and mean,
But then the buzzing built inside
And Tim began to clean.

The swirling feelings grew inside
His arms began to whiz,
He rushed and raced about the house
In a swirly twirly tiz.

He used his arms to wash and mop
And squish and splash and jangle;
But Tim was such a whirlwind
It ended in a tangle.

His arms were in a muddle;
Poor Tim let out a groan.
He'd tied himself all up in knots
And he was all alone.

He wriggled and he squiggled
And then let out a yelp;
He'd only made it worse
He knew he needed help.

He couldn't fix this by himself
No matter how he tried,
He'd need a friend to help him
He'd have to go outside.

Tim found Jenni playing,
She helped him right away.
"I'll help," she said, "with one request,
That afterwards you play."

"But everything's a mess," said Tim,
"I can't forget it's there."
"Well, how about we don't," she said,
"But right now let's not care.

"Let's just play together
Let's splash and play about;
And then when playtime's over
We'll go and sort it out.

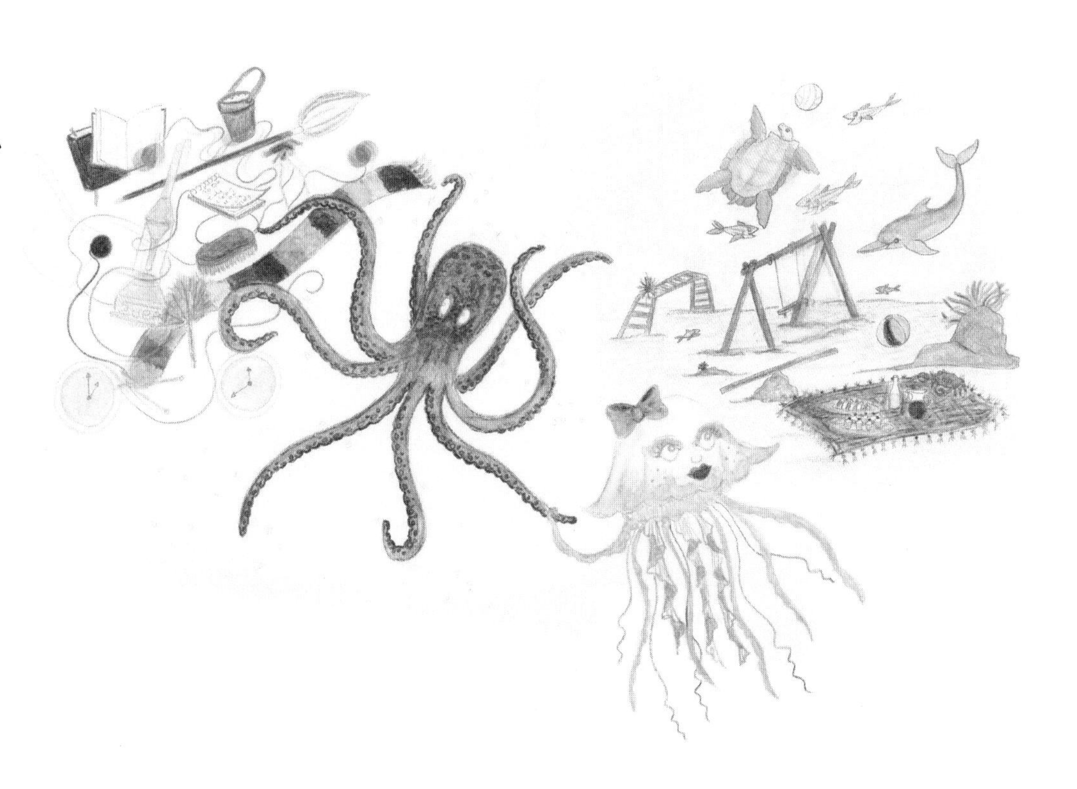

"And I can come and help you
That's if you want a friend;
My arms may not be as fast like yours
But mine are yours to lend.

"I might not be efficient
Or I might not be as strong;
But if we work together
It might not take as long.

"And if you want to carry on
And do things your own way,
I'll still pop by and think of you
And ask you out to out to play

"And you can always call me
If you're ever in a muddle,
And I'll be there to help you out
And offer you a cuddle."

With Jenni as his trusted friend
And her accepting him,
He saw what made him different
Also made him Tim!!

The tizzy feelings faded
As he realised, in the end,
He did not need more arms,
What he needed was a friend.

Tidy Tim – text only version

Deep, deep down in the ocean
Where squishy fishes swim,
Lived many different creatures
And an octopus called Tim.

Tim wasn't very friendly
Or blessed with many charms,
But Tim had lots of other skills
As well as lots of arms.

Tim was super organised
And always had a plan;
His house was very ordered
And always spick and span.

One day a knock came to his door,
He heard a small voice say,
“Hello, Tim – are you in there?
Oh, won’t you come and play?”

He looked out of his window
“It’s me,” a voice declared.
“It’s Jenni the jelly fish! Please come play!”
But Tim just stood and stared.

“I’m busy,” Tim replied at once
“I’ve lots of things to do
The house is very messy
I have no time for you”

Jenni asked Tim every day,
Though he never once came out
She'd ask him still, just in case,
And so he wouldn't feel left out.

Jenni turned and swam away
And Tim felt sad and mean,
But then the buzzing built inside
And Tim began to clean.

The swirling feelings grew inside
His arms began to whiz,
He rushed and raced about the house
In a swirly twirly tiz.

He used his arms to wash and mop
And squish and splash and jangle;
But Tim was such a whirlwind
It ended in a tangle.

His arms were in a muddle;
Poor Tim let out a groan.
He'd tied himself all up in knots
And he was all alone.

He wriggled and he squiggled
And then let out a yelp;
He'd only made it worse
He knew he needed help.

He couldn't fix this by himself
No matter how he tried,
He'd need a friend to help him
He'd have to go outside.

Tim found Jenni playing,
She helped him right away.
"I'll help," she said, "with one request,
That afterwards you play."

“But everything’s a mess,” said Tim,
“I can’t forget it’s there.”
“Well, how about we don’t,” she said,
“But right now let’s not care.

“Let’s just play together
Let’s splash and play about;
And then when playtime’s over
We’ll go and sort it out.

“And I can come and help you
That’s if you want a friend;
My arms may not be as fast like yours
But mine are yours to lend.

“I might not be efficient
Or I might not be as strong;
But if we work together
It might not take as long.

“And if you want to carry on
And do things your own way,
I’ll still pop by and think of you
And ask you out to out to play

“And you can always call me
If you’re ever in a muddle,
And I’ll be there to help you out
And offer you a cuddle.”

With Jenni as his trusted friend
And her accepting him,
He saw what made him different
Also made him Tim!!

The tizzy feelings faded
As he realised, in the end,
He did not need more arms,
What he needed was a friend.